PSALMS OF IRAQ

BY KENNETH J. BUTLER

The Psalms of Iraq
By: Kenneth J. Butler

Cover design by: Andre M. Saunders
Logo design by: Andre M. Saunders
Photography by: Kenneth J. Butler
Editor: ALisha Broughton
Associate Editor: Anelda L. Ballard

© 2008 Kenneth J. Butler
ISBN# 978-0-9768540-5-0
ISBN# 0-9768540-5-8

All rights reserved. This book is protected under the copyright laws of the United States of America. This book may not be copied or reprinted for commercial gain or profit. The use of short quotations or occasional page copying for personal or group study is permitted and encouraged. Permission will be granted upon request.

Scripture quotations are from the Maxwell Leadership Bible, King James Version, New King James Version, New International Version and the New Living Translation of the Holy Bible.

For Worldwide Distribution
Printed in the United States of America
Published by Jazzy Kitty Greetings Marketing & Publishing, LLC
Utilizing Microsoft Publishing Software

ACKNOWLEDGMENTS

Being part of God's kingdom has inspired me dearly has and kept me upright and true to myself. Since coming to the realization of the Psalms of my expressions. Foremost, I would like to thank God for Psalms and love for the word to place in this book. I have a heart for people to see and hear their own Psalms through mine. I would like to thank God for the safety and courage that has been placed in my spirit while traveling to other countries. I would like to acknowledge Bishop Emma L. Creamer from the Cathedral of Fresh Fire, where the Pentecostal flames are always burning. She has steered my Psalms to know thyself and inspired me to pray more than usual. Prayers work and are proven in the way you pray and live. First guidance from her is like receiving the love to share with others. She taught me that the bible was the only infallible word from God. There is not enough love and words to express the kind of woman Pastor Creamer is and the love she has given. I tell you when she baptized me I felt a difference then and vowed to pray and honor God to the fullest extent. Regardless if I attended her church or not, she would always be a guiding planet for me to grow from. Thank you Pastor! My mother Helen Butler is courageous in her own steps showing strength through her trials. She encouraged me to keep it up and take my time in whatever I do. I also thank God for giving me the courage to conquer what I thought I feared and that was being in a war zone. I also would like to thank the commanders and soldiers of 1/150th Aviation unit, we have completed a tour for eighteen months together. Besides that I have found an angel and this angel is proven to me to be a destined vision in this Psalms. Seeing my vision made clear through the Prophetess made this complete. Finally, I would like to acknowledge the General Taluto of the 42nd Infantry Division, working under his staff was a great experience.

DEDICATIONS

I dedicate this book to the soldiers who have the art of Psalms within them. This is not a lesson learned manual for us, but a form of acknowledgment within to find the words within themselves. Place them within their hearts and creates the Psalms of Life.

This will bring out loving attitudes for others to respect. This is a fine awareness to see the love inside. The words will and can spill from your lips and into the hearts of others.

TABLE OF CONTENTS

Introduction	....	i
Chapter 1	About Time...	1
Chapter 2	Cell Block P.O.L.................................	6
Chapter 3	New Land...	13
Chapter 4	FOB Danger..	26
Chapter 5	Fresh Fire...	37
Chapter 6	Completing the End.............................	45
Pictures	Pictures of Iraq....................................	52

INTRODUCTION

When people think of Psalms they think of King David, King Solomon and the sons of Korah, Asaph, Heman, Ethan, and a handful of anonymous writers. Psalms show actions and feeling that reflect human emotions. Bible readers through the ages have flocked to the Book of Psalms. Its poetic words reflect the entire range of human emotions. Therefore, Psalms of Iraq reflect the emotions I have encountered through the OIF3 (Operation Iraqi Freedom) encountered all sorts of emotions, some good, some sad. The moods that I experienced in Iraq embrace the whole range of human experience from exuberant praise Psalm 145 to despair Psalm 42; from intense anger Psalm 137 and doubt about God's care Psalm 73; to hope for a future based precisely upon God's care Psalm 23. They help us express emotions that otherwise we might not have words for, or feel right about. Psalms catches the reality of our up-and down relationship with God, but they move us steadily along the path of knowing God.

The Psalms of Iraq is my collection of emotions and thoughts viewed from situations felt within the realm of God's hand and hold. I like the various writers of Psalms aim to express my deepest feelings and longings as well as the truth of God's wisdom. These ancient Hebrew songs contribute to our understanding of definitive and dynamic ways. They are definitive because they contain God's thoughts and values. They help me and others understand how God thinks, what he values and how he might respond to certain circumstance regarding life's circle. They are dynamic because they explore our ups-and-downs of a person's emotion. David, who wrote the majority of Psalm, expressed every emotion he felt as a servant of God's Word. The joy of God's victories, to the deep contribution for his sin and

INTRODUCTION

Shortcomings. We all have to introduce ourselves to our emotions and relate them to our Psalms in our lives. Some Psalms are communal or personal expressions of thanksgiving, lament, or moral dilemma. I had to live a life under emotions ranging from all sorts of feelings under circumstances while in another country. Being faced with danger all sorts of thoughts surfaced and gained sight through the Book of Psalms. The Book of Psalms was actually living in Iraq. God was constructing and building the PSALMS OF IRAQ in me. We all have a Psalm or Psalms with us, find God and you will find your PSALMS. Know yourself and you will know your PSALMS. Know God and you will know your PSALMS!

CHAPTER 1

ABOUT TIME

God has a way of proving himself to others in ways where you will see the effects after the situation. A situation sometimes enhances a person's ability to see and react to God's presence, and that is what people need in their lives "Situations". The United States encountered situations that effected millions especially the military. People predicting the coming of a new age, which was the end of 1999 and the coming of 2000. Everyone was thinking "THE END". However, it is actually the beginning of so many situations that the world would least expect. Therefore the world and country slipped the 2000 was shaken, not knowing the expectations of any sort. Then 2001, we were hit at the WTC (World Trade Center) and the Pentagon, and all things broke loose around the country and the military was called to arms. The threat level was raised and the shield was put up. It affected all branches of the military.

Since I was in the Delaware Army National Guard, it did not hit us until May of 2004. Everyone in the National Guard knew before hand like in February 2004, this is what I meant about situations arising and realizing after the fact. Therefore the preparation for Deployment of OIF3 (Operation Iraqi Freedom) began. Actually we had been preparing for war, this is what the National Guard does, prepare for all things. So, I thought I must be preparing myself for God's glory. 1 Corinthians 10:23 (Maxwell Leadership Bible) All things are lawful for me, but all things are helpful; all things are lawful for me, but not all things edify. Showing everything is permissible-but not everything is beneficial, everything is permissible-but not everything is constructive. God is permitting us to enter into new boundaries and do His glory; a job needs to be performed. In addition, through God's grace, I will complete whatever God has me to do, this was my thought while preparing. What could be on the minds of the loved ones? This was the time to be more loving to each other and support each other. Families definitely need family support. Soldiers were offered classes which enabled them and their families to prepare for the departure. So, the classes began and the prepping for support began. Knowing how to cope with your loved one and going to an imminent danger zone or away. It rather reminds me of the ancient days of war. Soldiers going away to war and the families watching along the lines.

In May 2004, the unit we were detached to was HHC (Headquarter Headquarters Company) $1/150^{TH}$ AVN BN, GSAB, (General Supply Aviation Battalion), where we had to become part of more units from New Jersey, Indiana, Missouri, New York, and Michigan to become a whole Battalion for the 42nd Infantry Division. This kind of structure grew to fifteen thousand (15,000) strong. The structure was simple we had Division, Battalion, Company, Section, Platoon, and self that is our chain all down to one. 1 Corinthians 12:12 (KJV) For as the body is one and hath many members and all the members of that one body, being many is one body. Verse 14, For the body is not one member, but many. In addition, we became many. That was our division, and one body. It was kind of strange meeting new people and to think they were supposed to have our backs during war. It was not as if they were our friends or anything like that, but eventually the love grew. Shucks! Remember the saying "I wouldn't go to war with you". These were people we never met before and now depending on them to look out for us and vice versa. Thus the building of friendships begun in no time. God builds things in relationships to make things happen. Proverbs 18:24 (KJV) A man that hath friends must shew himself friendly: and there is a friend that sticketh closer than a brother. Therefore, these soon to be war brothers have just been enlisted to our souls as brothers. We were in this thing all together for this rainbow division 42nd Infantry Division. We began our training in Fort Dix, New Jersey for five months of training and preparation which was somewhat hard but understandable to the fullest extent. We learned everything from weather conditions, to how to protect an army post or should I say FOB (Forward Operating Base). I guess since we were entering new land and boundaries we had to know it. Building up our own faith spiritually, mentally and physically, I am saying this because some soldiers were still weak from leaving home. Therefore their thoughts and hearts were not in it, meaning maybe they were not ready for this deployment. It would leave them physically weak, but I guess the army thought it would take five months to build up the moral, which consist of spirit, mental and physical character. To be truthful, due to the fact everyone was broken and defeated before we even left the country. It was difficult to build up moral. It consisted of training and more training. We trained like I prayed everyday, yeah we had days off, but the next day we went over what we missed the day before. Some soldiers trained with a purpose and created new goals and healthy spirits. Romans 8:28-30 (KJV) states: We know that all things work for good for those who love God, to them who are called according to His purpose. Verse 29, For whom He did foreknow, He also did predestinate to be conformed to the image of His son, that he might be the firstborn among many brethren. Verse 30, Moreover whom He did predestinate, then He is also called; and whom He called them shall be also justified; and whom He justified shall be glorified. Therefore we had men and woman soldiers putting all out in training. Soldiers were showing they were predestined to be here and they regained strength and were glorified in God. But as for me, I put God in everything I did and was renewed. That showed me everyone else did also, even if they did not act like it.

We trained for the weather since history shows temperatures of 120 to 140 were relevant degrees in Iraq. We trained for hot weather conditions wearing the helmet Kevlar which weighed 40 pounds on our bodies. Temperatures, in Fort Dix were 90 degrees this could actually hurt someone. We trained using the weapons, firing all kinds of weapons to familiarize ourselves with them. Then soldiers split into teams and did guard duty of a FOB (Forward Operating Base) post. People were acting like Iraqi civilians being irate and protesting. This was all training, and we had to detain them. Mind you all this was under heat conditions. The days were long and nights were short. Too short for all the training, short nights meant less sleep, but the training went on.

Division Main Building (Saddam Mother Palace)

CHAPTER 2

CELL BLOCK P.O.L

Everyone was categorized by section regardless of what state you were from. Remember we were training with New Jersey Guard, Missouri Guard, Michigan Guard, and New York Guard. All types of MOS's (Military Occupational Specialty) job, everyone was sectioned off by their Military Occupational Specialty (MOS). I was 92F, POL Aviation Refueler. This is a job where we refuel everything that flies. I meant everything and this was also part of the training, to do the training under all the conditions. The Delaware Guard was roomed with New Jersey and Missouri and all of us had the same job (MOS). The building was 1528, Second Floor, Room 210.

We were twelve to thirteen strong in our section, thus so the comraderie began, fellowshipping and friendships formed, like how Christ formed the disciples. All became friends and did everything together and formed them from His glory. We became one, thirteen men in one room, learning each others ways and tactics, pulling pranks and jokes on each other and most of all looking after each others backs. We became a team as in Luke 9:10-17, the soldiers became strong and were able to complete such a task of feeding thousands of people. I am sure they dealt with all kinds' of attitudes and situations of certain people to feed. We had our pranks and jokesters to pass the time away.

Then came the dreadful time when they placed the whole company on lock down. No one could get a pass or leave the post. Some people felt like they were in prison. Our POL section came up with cell block P.O.L, just to be funny.

One morning we were called to formation where Officers would call out individual names when they came to one of our sections guys names, he would scream out loud and clear "CELL BLOCK POL". This went on for at least a day or so, and then we were asked to stop. Therefore, we had to direct our humor on each other. Our room had some home comfort accommodations such as a, TV, VCR, DVD, Play Station and a bunch of games to play with, yeah what a deployment! We made each other feel welcomed and loving, whether we knew it or not. Some had hard times being confined to a room with twelve people, tempers flaring and arguments arose. We still were going to another country and training continued. Did I mention we had two females in our section; they had their own room. They never knew how much fun we had in our room. These two females in our section were dedicated soldiers in the army; both driven to complete a mission endured by all the training with us. The men accepted them as sisters of P.O.L. and looked out for them like ourselves. They endured the pranks as the men did. I am sure they heard, the pranks kept most of us sane and stable, but we never took our mind off the mission at hand. You have to realize when you are determined in the spirit, you are determined in your heart. Fort Dix started to become full soldiers coming from all over the country and really forming the 42nd Division, which around the world is known as the "RAINBOW DIVISION". They were from upstate New York the Albany area, so the majority of the Division was from there and the New York City area. I love God and how the division formed, formed in my sense. I was constantly thinking of how God could make this deployment good for me while going through all the trials and situations.

If you can remember Joseph and his brothers, well it's the reunion of love, and the power of God working on both sides. I mention this due to the fact; I met some old army buddies from the New York area, they were from Brooklyn. They were still in the military. Let me say, I was in the New York Guard prior to being in the Delaware Guard. I was attached to the 42nd S&T

Battalion from Brooklyn, New York, a Supply and Transport Unit. I saw several people from my old unit and Wow! God works in some good ways to bring them in my life for a brief moment of the deployment. Who would have known I would see them again.

We all trained under the same division. This training lasted about five months at Fort Dix. One of the grueling and intensive training was the convoy training. We had maneuvered under serious fire and danger; we were put in desert situations, and moving under direct fire and returning fire. Our crew POL stood strong amongst the people, we had built a sort of unity amongst us Ephesians 4:1-8 reads: I, therefore, the prisoner of the Lord, beseech you walk worthy of the calling with which you were called, with all lowliness and gentleness, with longsuffering, bearing with one another in love, endeavoring to keep the unity of the spirit in the bond of peace. There is one body and one spirit, just as you were called in the hope of your calling; one Lord, one faith, one baptism; one God and father of all, who is above all, and through all and in you all. But each one of us grace was given according to the measure of Christ gift; therefore He says "when He ascended on high, He led captivity captive, and gave gifts to men." So each of us deployed our gifts to show and get by the grueling task we all had to face in training. God I thank you for the gift of strength.

All through the training I had to create a Psalms within me. Being at Fort Dix was an eye opening experience for what was to come for us. The days became closer for us to leave and head out for our Iraqi adventure. The soldiers started doing crazy outrageous things for instance like: going AWOL, partying, and fights broke out amongst the soldiers, and the brigade placed everyone on lock, so people were punished even if they did not do anything. I remember Jeremiah. Jeremiah declares that God's way of punishing His people is by giving them bad leaders. Our ranking officers were punishing people who had or had not done anything to get punished for. Which most of us thought was wrong. Jeremiah 30:10-11 (Maxwell Leadership Bible) Therefore do not fear, O my servant Jacob says the Lord, nor be dismayed, O Israel; for behold, I will save you from afar, and your seed from the land of their captivity. Jacob shall return, have rest and be quiet, and no one shall make him afraid. For I am with you, says the Lord to save you; though I make full end of all nations where I have scattered you. Yet, I will not make a complete end of you. I will correct you in justice, and I will not let you go unpunished.

Everything rises and falls on the leadership, they were called to lead and people were messing up and some were getting blamed. Soldiers were looking out for friends doing bad things, because they actually found ways of getting out. I guess as long as their friends were looking out they were good to go. The spirit of God sort of always existed in our room, giving us the fruits of our joy. We had the luxury of the goods and did not have to go out abroad and get in any trouble. Some nights were harder for some of us, due to the fact some of the guys were older than the rest. Men were getting sick, men had heart problems, but the mission went on.

Men did not want to get sent home for anything less than being hurt. We had a soldier, who was so sick, and the fact that he did not want to leave was intriguing to me, plus he was in our section POL (Petroleum Oils and Lubricants). Now that is soldier dedication to the fullest, and was devoted to the section as a whole, his commitment and daring courage to our vision comes out of Isaiah 63 verses 11 through 14, then he remembered the days of old, Moses and his people saying; "Where is He who brought them up out of the sea, with the shepherd of his flock?" Where is He who put His Holy Spirit within him? Who led them by the right hand of Moses with His glorious arm, dividing the water before them to make for Himself an everlasting name, who led them through the deep, as a horse in the wilderness that they might not stumble? As a beast goes down into the valley, and the Spirit of the Lord causes him to rest, so you lead your people, to make yourself a glorious name. Isaiah recalls that Moses received his courage from his God-given convictions. Moses relationship with God came first; next came a foundation of convictions; and finally the courage. This also showed me devotion of this Soldier, a heart filled with love of fellow soldiers. Just as Jesus was devoted to healing souls, some soldiers were devoted to staying regardless of their own physical mishaps. The God in me provided direction to a soldier and he continued on to Iraq.

It had to be around 1:30 am, everyone sleeping in the whole barracks, one soldier in my section came over to my bunk, now our room is pitch dark, so dark. I heard a voice in the dark saying "Butler, Butler". At first, I did not know who or what was going on, thought I was dreaming or something. The voice became closer to my bed, funny thing I was feeling the dark with my hands reaching for the voice, like a blind man walking. Then I realized who it was, so I jumped out of the bed frantically asking, "You don't need me to go with you to the Men's room, HUH"? Do you? He said, "No", but you may need to get SFC Shortlidge, who is our section chief. Now this man is a great leader and has placed a great influence on me and a lot of fellows in our section. I ran to get SFC Shortlidge and came back to the soldier asking questions trying to place the problem. Chest pains was his reply and shortness of breath, so Fort Dix ambulance was called and responded quite fast, well the situation awoke the whole building. Taking my man out, I had the question in my head "Why was I chosen to help?" I was tired and sleepy. I wondered what God's view was on the whole thing. You never know how and where God will place you for assistance and put you in the position to assist others. I was praying every night reading my word and obeying the

Spirit of God. 1 John 3:23 (KJV) And this is His commandment, That we should believe on the name of His Son Jesus Christ, and love one another, as He gave us commandment. I felt sort of responsible. Titus 3:1 (KJV) Put them in mind to be subject to principalities and powers, to obey magistrates, to be ready to every good work. Titus 3:4 (KJV) But after that the kindness and love of God our Savior toward man appeared, was shown towards the soldier. It appeared towards this soldier in the need of assistance from God, which appeared through me. God is so awesome in our time of need. My commandment was to assist in getting help and guidance for the soldier. So the soldier went to the hospital and we all thought, OH well another one gone home, but not him. He came back saying "I can't leave you guys." Now that is devotion! Devotion described in a realistic fashion. All the guys in our section looked at the soldier differently with more courage in thought; he was determined to complete the tour with us. Now that is true courage, completing something and disregarding your own health. Psalms has spoken though assistance.

THE DESERTS OF IRAQ
THINK ABOUT THE DESERTS IN OUR LIVES

CHAPTER 3

NEW LAND

The day came for us to depart from Fort Dix, NJ. Some happy and some sad, some ready and some excited. But the day approached clear as day, emotions ran all over the place. God had prepared us for this day in advance and this was the beginning of what God had prepared for us. Individuals had to conquer the fact that the day is here. Patience was turned instantly into strength Psalm 40:1-2 (KJV) I waited patiently for The Lord: and He inclined unto to me, and He heard my cry. He brought me out of the miry clay and set my feet upon a rock and established my goings. Everyone had some sort of patience, since the training was so tough and intense and then finally getting the word to leave the post. For me, I was preparing for the level in which I was headed. My prayers went up to God to instill in me the courage to withstand the next plateau. We were about to embark on new ground, everyone needs to know how it feels to go somewhere they never been, that is pure love and strength known to God.

So the day of November 11, 2004 came and it was like something that was waiting in my heart to approach. It seemed like everyone's purpose became their passion Deuteronomy 4:40 (KJV) Thou shalt keep therefore His statues and His commandments, which I have command thee this day, and it may go well with thee and thy children after thee, and thou mayest prolong thy days upon the earth, which The Lord hath given thee forever. Saying yeah they were ready with a passion as long as they kept his commandment and obeyed God's word. The faces of the unknown were on a lot of people's faces, not knowing what to expect from this day forward. Thinking we did train enough for this mission, we did learn enough for this. Remembering Psalm 46:1-3 (KJV) God is our refuge and strength, a very present help in trouble. Therefore will not we fear, though the earth be removed, the mountains be carried into the midst of the sea; though the waters thereof roar and be troubled, though the mountains shake with the swelling thereof. So, I thought if a world can withstand all this a person can withstand the trials of facing new land.

    The flight was amazing now God was in sync with my reality. You fly through a time zone, like a time warp and the days move ahead or backward. Like time moving slowly, but actually moving at a time warp speed, enough speed to move us ahead a day or so. Putting oneself in God's hands are the most amazing feelings to feel. That is what I felt flying through the clouds. Then I read Psalm 27 that actually blessed my soul. Thinking about the arrival to Kuwait. Psalm 27 verses 1 through 3 states, The Lord is my light and my salvation whom shall I fear? The Lord is the strength of my life; of whom shall I be afraid? When the wicked, even mine enemies and my foes, came upon me to eat up my flesh, they stumbled and fell. Though an host should encamp against me, my heart shall not fear: though war should rise against me, in this I will be confident. I built up my confidence with the 27th Psalms of David. I didn't know the enemies or foes, but I had confidence and was not afraid to enter the stronghold of the enemy. The comfort of the Lord set in me throughout the whole flight. Funny thing was that, upon arriving I was thinking about my luggage like I was traveling United Airlines or some commercial flight or something. When we arrived in Kuwait, you could smell the different country and sound of new land. I asked my battle buddy (Joe Jennings), "Where are we getting our bags." Joe said, "I don't know." but we were told later after we arrived. Now Joe is a head strong, firefighter, head of a record label from Chester, PA, ex-marine turned Army kind of guy. He was very comical in our room and had everyone cracking up laughing with his Bernie Mac impressions. Joe and I became close since Fort

Dix. Therefore, we stuck together; some people need to understand one of the greatest friendships examples in the bible is that of David and Jonathan Saul's Son. 1 Samuel 18 verse 3, speaks on the friendship of David and Jonathan. They were friends under crazy circumstances and conditions. We became close under war conditions and looked out for each other. For if you seen me, you seen Joe. The training became more advanced in Kuwait, since we were in Kuwait for a month; we spent Christmas in Kuwait, which was different for most of us. Sleeping habits became off and training became intense and long. More convoy training and we became broken down by squads and sections, more meetings and very early mornings.

    Safety became an issue for the entire training taken place and thought of doing the right thing was running in everyone's minds. Thinking if they did the task in a safe manner will they be alright. Convoy training was different, due to the fact we had to learn to follow the vehicle in front of us in the sand and dust. I received a lot of satisfaction from God in my time of training Psalm 17:15 (KJV) As for me I will behold thy face in righteousness: I shall be satisfied, when I awake, with thy likeness. Making all things glorified in the face of God, regardless of all distractions. So every night I lay my head awake, I will be satisfied to see the face of my creator and give Him thanks. Psalm 107:9 (NKVJ) For He satisfies the longing soul, and fills the hungry soul with goodness. God had satisfied my soul through thick and thin and kept me filled with His goodness. Let me say that in Kuwait, our whole platoon was placed in a tent which held 30 to 35 people, that is 30 to 35 different personalities. So God kept me filled with His goodness through all the different people and attitudes. But Joe had the personality of a good man, with Godly intentions. Therefore, we decided to make it through together cause the guys in this tent was kind of wild nothing like the room in Fort Dix. But, I am thinking am I the only sane person? Everyone is probably thinking the same thing. Therefore, here we were dealing with soldiers personalities in a new land and thinking about the next level of this deployment. Therefore, another level of patience kicked in. That is when I realized patience has certain levels. I have been waiting patiently for The Lord and strength to deal with these different people in my circle. I know I have been asking for God to give me patience and guidance on what and how to deal with the deployment situations. We were in CAMP BUERHRING, Kuwait; the temperature was hot reaching 100 to 130 degrees and by night going to 85 to 90, shucks still hot. When the holidays came around like Thanksgiving and Christmas, the thought of home set in the heart and spirit hit pretty hard for us.

Everyone wanted to be home and some folks started acting out on it. The army makes up for the away feeling by feeding us great food, like steak and lobster for the holidays. Everyone knows how to get a person to forget his troubles, feed him some good food. Soldiers did not care; they would wait in lines as long as 200 to 300 people. If you wanted to eat you had to get in line early. Sometimes, the lines were too long to go to breakfast. Therefore, we would skip breakfast, and maybe lunch and dinner. When we found out about the Burger King Stand it was all over. Burgers everyday because they reminded us of home.

One of the better challenges I had was keeping myself sane and faithful to God's word. I had people trying my patience with God Psalm 39:1 (KJV) I will take heed to my ways that I sin not with my tongue: I will keep my mouth with a bridle, while the wicked is before me. Being around other people with cruel and funny ways can sometimes rub off on a person. Being around different personalities had me watch them closer than ever, we are here not to judge others but to guide and love them as Jesus loved us.

The sense of working together kicked in full blast over the weeks in

Kuwait. The word came down that we would be leaving Camp Buerhring, Kuwait and we would be driving into Iraq via convoy and it would take three days, but we had no armor on our trucks, so we had to make and add our own armor. Very interesting task, which meant we had no protection. Therefore, we were preparing again in a different sense, we began our physical structure for protection. I began to think about preparing in Fort Dix, NJ and preparing in Kuwait.

A likeness between things, when things are otherwise entirely different. For instance, "Learning is to the mind what is light to the eye," enabling it to discover hidden things. So what I am expressing is the difference in learning the compassion of preparing for protection. Our fuel trucks needed armor those trucks were for the aircrafts we support, they were carrying two hundred and five hundred thousand (2,500) gallons per truck and we had six. Therefore, we needed doors and some sort of protection in case we get hit from enemy fire in our convoy. Working day and night was no option for us. We took care of the doors and made protection the best way we knew how and had the vehicles covered. God blessed us with the ingenuity to create protection on our own, I felt like I had a new job (welder). When all the vehicles were done, the word was out, we were ready to leave. Then you felt the grumbling of people because we actually were leaving, different kind of feeling from Fort Dix.

Listening to God was a key for me. You had to know your surroundings to keep the peace with yourself. Psalm 5:11 (KJV) But let all those that put their trust in thee rejoice: let them ever shout for joy, because thou defendest them: let them also that love thy name be joyful in thee. Rejoicing in the name of The Lord was very important to me and the people who praise His name in times of trouble or mishaps. We were about to go into new land and everyone was being adjustable to our new journey. Asking for protection from God was my priority in this case. It was like everything we trained and learned came down to this, even spiritual training. Everything we been through came to this, praying and thinking of arriving at our destination in Tikrit, Iraq. So my battle buddy Joe Jennings and our section was pretty calm, cause we all stayed in the same tent, laughter and fun kept some people sane, some people prayed and stayed to themselves. Some people could not sleep and stayed up all-night long.

The morning came for us to load our gear and equipment, then a safety briefing from our commander about the route we were taking, saying we will be making three stops for rest and only drive by day and rest by night, I guess traveling by day was the safest for the convoy of three 3 serials and twenty trucks each serial. Everyone was paired off, driver and assistant driver, some trucks had gunners, but we all had live rounds for the 16A1 rifle, five magazines each for each soldier. I was driving the Hemtt Fuel Truck (Heavy Equipment Military Tactical Truck) with an assistant driver. The feeling of a different kind started to run through my mind and body, thinking this was about to happen, enter into Iraq and actually drive three days. The thought of entering another country became strange, since I was always told to be invited before entering another person's house. I told my assistant I was going to pray with him for us. I prayed Psalm 18:1-3 (NKJV) I will love you O Lord, my strength. The Lord is my rock and my fortress and my deliverer; My God, my strength, in whom will I trust; my shield and the horn of my salvation, my stronghold. I will call upon the Lord, who is worthy to be praised; so shall I be saved from my enemies. I was basically putting us in the line to be covered by the shield of righteousness. As long as we are right in the heart and exact in the mind we shall be protected by God and His angels.

So our journey began of three days in the afternoon of December 27,

2004, where we would leave "Camp Buerhring", Kuwait, we traveled along this road and night fell upon us. I think we traveled about 60 to 70 miles and came to our first rest stop "NAVISTAR". Navistar means to navigate through the stars, it felt like we have been driving for days, but it was only hours. I guess since the convoy was driving 15 to 20 miles per hour, very slow. Therefore, by the time we hit Navistar rest stop it was pitch dark, but very interesting; we pulled out cots and sleeping bags and set up outdoor sleeping quarters. First we had to get some chow from the mess hall. The food was great buffet style for the soldiers all you can eat. Ribs to steaks, crabmeat to lobsters the food was awesome. I thank God for a great meal, due to the fact of not knowing if there was another meal like that coming forth. That night felt funny, since sleeping under trucks. The night was cool and the temperature dropped to 50 or 60 degrees. Hey, that is considered cold because our bodies were getting adjusted to the weather over there. One of my main thoughts was as we sleep, who is going to watch guard. Navistar is on the border line of the Kuwaiti and Iraqi border. So trusting in God while I rested on the border became kind of an issue for me at night. Psalm 16:1 (KVJ) states: Preserve me O God: for in thee do I put my trust. Yes, I have always put my trust in my Lord, and this was a true act of it. Shucks! I know people are sneaky and this is their land and they know the in and outs to getting around the lines. The 16th Psalms of David dwelled in my spirit. Praying for my Lord to keep me safe while I rest in the night air. As I lay in the night, I felt like Navistar was a point to reach to begin another journey. The stars were bright like guidance for us. They were so bright and kind of close; you could have reached up, and grabbed one and had your very own star to assist you.

    The next morning was a day of grace for us all. We all gave thanks for a peaceful rest in Navistar, which I named a place for stars. Then we were all called to the next safety meeting to begin the journey towards the next rest stop. I placed the shield of protection on again as usual and mounted in the truck. The drive was amazing; the view of the country side of Iraq was a plain level. You can easy wander off while driving, but we had to combine a few things together, driving with safety and drifting off into the empty land of danger. The land looked so empty but full of potential danger towards us. The danger was actually leering out at us and driving we couldn't even see them, but getting to our destination was our purpose. My inner strength became my determination shown on the outside. Psalm 20:2-4 (KVJ) Send thee help from the sanctuary, (my heart or my church family, prayers) and strengthen thee out of Zion; Verse 3, Remember all thy offering, and accept thy burnt sacrifices; Selah. Verse 4, Grant thee according to thine own heart and fulfill all thy counsel. Actually the help from within came from God, My heart and soul is thy sanctuary and God had strengthen it while I was driving. I was granted strength from God according to my heart and determination. We had to reach the next rest stop, without any casualties.

While driving along the road which looked like a rugged I-95 interstate, we were encountering a lot of empty land. What really intrigued me were the kids. Kids were all over the road for miles and miles asking for food or anything we had. Our trucks kept on going non-stop. The visibility was clear and you could see for miles, and these kids came out of nowhere and they looked like ages from 1 to 7 years of age all along the road. Further down the road were the older kids ranging from 12 to 17 years old and were throwing rocks and debris at our trucks as we rode by. Shoot! Everyone donned a weapon even the cooks, they were handy with a M16. You never know what to expect driving along those kinds of roads trying not to sleep or nod. Once you have nodded something has happened. Traveling mercy was my prayer for three long days, praying for God to be near at all times was a normal action for me. Psalm 22:11 (KJV) Be not far from me; for trouble is near; for there is none to help. So traveling along the tuff roads of Iraq was a different kind of travel, instead of tall buildings and green pastures, you saw poverty stricken building torn land and children coming out of the ground and huts made of muck and mud. You know you see certain conditions in these situations and you wonder about the normal everyday living for these people. Where is the store? I asked myself and my assistant driver. Where do they get groceries? Normal questions for the everyday person. Where do they get the food? Questions like that ran through my mind for some distance. Why isn't anybody helping them? I felt sort of upset and sad at the same time. I asked The Lord those questions while driving. Psalm 37 verses 17 and 18, kept ringing in my spirit regarding the situation. For the arms of the wicked shall be broken: but the Lord upholdeth the righteous. The Lord knoweth the days of the upright: and their inheritance shall be forever. So I actually found that they shall prevail through all this, through God's grace and mercy. They shall be taken from the stronghold of the wicked and be shown to the world as the righteous. We arrived at another rest stop to shower but it was pitch dark and the water was so cold, shucks! We in America know the water as being crystal clear; it was so dark you didn't know if the water was brown or black, just wet. So all we did was get wet and hit the road again. To see the people again was definitely a reminder of what not to do and be in America and be forever glorified in God's sight, so I will always be blessed. I knew the people here in these conditions had to be praying every night, because they are still living as examples to others to be blessed. They struggle just like people in America and around the globe. Psalm 22:26 (NKJV) The poor shall eat and be satisfied; those who seek Him will praise the Lord. Let your heart live forever! This got me to really thinking the poor people are forever satisfied when they get morsels of food.

So it was only right for me to ask God to bless these children out here running around with no family, and looking for soldiers to give them food. Some soldiers gave and were throwing their food out to the kids, and some did not, actually when you watch children go without you feel guilty inside. The bible says in Luke 6 verse 38 Give, and it will be given unto you: good measure, pressed down, shaken together, and running over will be put into your bosom. For with the same measure that you use, it will be measured back to you. So He had been preparing a table for them in a time of despair. Driving along roads not yet made was deep; we hit an unimproved highway along a stretch of miles. The following of trucks was great until the lead vehicle made a wrong turn into the city of Baghdad. It looked weird twenty or more military vehicles turning around in a large city town square, but it was done with no problem from the town's people, but they sure looked at us kind of funny. We were back on the road to this bombed out I-95. There were potholes as big as craters and the cracks in the ground lasted two miles or so. So our convoy driving skills were kicking with favor. I often thought of home while driving thinking of my then wife Darlene, what she is doing right at the moment, was she asleep, working, or was she thinking about me as well. It always happened when I was wondering to another peaceful place. The convoy had stopped in the middle of the road and stood still for a few minutes or so. Our first sergeant came walking the line of vehicles telling every one to dismount and hit the side of the tires and cover for protection. I was thinking to myself, "Okay, action" something is going on. Mind you, I have on protective gear that weighs forty pounds or so, a Kevlar helmet and ammo pouches with live ammo. We had to act on response. Therefore, I had to hop down from the truck, lay next to the driver side of the wheel pointing outward, and so was everyone else. Training was so well done. So we laid there for around 15 to 20 minutes. They came back saying all clear, come to find out there was an IED in the road in front of the lead vehicle. IED stands for improved, explosive device. For which they were placing in everything from garbage to dead animals. God is a God of wonders, protection over our whole convoy. Psalm 77:14 (KJV) Thou art the God that doest wonders: thou hast declared thy strength among the people. He should show the wonders of love in an aspect of detection he detected the road bomb, before we rode by. Thank you Lord! I spoke about that all the way to my assistant, making sure he sees the truth of the power of God. Only GOD can detect and protect you from the things unseen. The next rest stop was a quick sleep and go type of thing nothing outrageous refuel our trucks and on the road. Days of driving seemed endless; driving along these long stretches of roads seemed we were coming to no end. Then, it was time to switch drivers and then I felt like yeah! I might see some action for a change. Riding with the M16 out the window at the ready position. When nothing was happening it became kind of boring, boring rides makes a person sleepy and tired, but we couldn't even nod for a second. My driver and I began to know each other, and did I mention no bathrooms to use just keep driving. We started describing our lives back home, SPC. Reno Reali was his name a very giving individual; he had a wife back home and new baby. He was all the attitude a person needs to get a motivated feeling. He would try and muster up feelings for everyone else and go and do everything even if the person did not want it. He did it! Reno and I talked about family issues while driving so it can pass the time away and not look at nothing in the desert. I was thinking this is actually war we are in. We are actually driving in the war zone, with a fuel truck no fuel yet, but we still have a fuel truck, big eye opener for the enemy. I started explaining something to Reno. He was only 21 and me being his fathers age, I felt a duty to minister a word, our Job we are called to here is simple, like how Jesus said in John 9 verse 4, I must work the works of him that sent me, while it is day: the night cometh, when no man can work. We will work all day I told him and rest by night so we can have strength for the next day, the Lord knows that he sent us here to do a mission for the military, right now is driving. But we all made it without falling asleep at the wheel. We thank God for traveling mercy, for he has kept us strong and awake for the time, aware of any danger before us; we give God all the Glory!

THOUGHTS ON THE EDGE

CHAPTER 4

FOB DANGER

Upon arriving in Camp Speicher, we had our Blackhawks bring us in. It seemed kind of cool as we followed them in from the ground, and they were protecting us from the air, and watching the area from the air. We arrived in the new FOB, (Forwarding Operating Base) which we were to be there for the duration of our whole tour. This was a giant Base; therefore, we pulled in and were greeted by our commander standing there like Moses when they crossed the sea. He was standing giving us courage and strength waving and all. As soon as we hit the FOB the screams and yells of happiness was clear and shouting "we made it, we made it!" I guess some people thought we were going to get hit. Didn't they know who was protecting us; sure wasn't the Blackhawk's flying over us guiding us in. It was all God's doing for that as well. Psalm 7 verse 10 says, My defense is of God, which saveth the upright in heart. That was our defense and protection from God. It was a blessed sight to see them fly over us and direct us to the base.

This I said was my next point, "Everyone in their life has a point to reach before moving on to the next one." This was my next one before the next one. We reached Iraq's point of growth, we now had to grow up and get adjusted to this place for the next twelve months. People were assigned their bunks and rooms, which happened to be metal containers turned into rooms. Therefore, you had to make to the best of your area to live in. Some containers held three or four people, some held two depending on the person, or who was friends with whom. Really, I did not care who they paired me with as long as I had a container with a bed and wall locker. A place, I can call home for twelve months. We had the formation and roll call to assure everyone was there in one piece. Also in the formation they (the commander and first sergeant) were letting everyone know the duties and assignments while on FOB Speicher. This is what I mean by God always looks out for the children of God, making a way for the blessed one, and I was ready to rejoice in formation. Since I felt like I was in right relationship with God, things were shining for me on that day for a reason. Matthew 6:6 (KJV) But thou, when thou prayest, enter into thy closet, and when thou hast shut thy door, pray to thy Father, which is in secret; and thy Father which seeth in secret shall reward thee openly. Hey, I felt I was getting a reward openly. Since, I prayed all the while going to and from, God had rewarded me greatly. I was told I was being assigned to a task at the palace and would be working under the Division General of the 42nd ID (Infantry Division). While the rest of our P.O.L section was going North of Iraq in Kirkuk, but we were going to be on his staff and sleep in the palace (one of Saddam's Palaces). I did not show my joy, because I didn't know what to expect there and my security. I was over excited and had the opportunity to choose who I wanted to work with me. I choose my battle buddy (Joe Jennings) the person who I became close to in Fort Dix. Yeah, Joe and I, we had to locate our bags and stuff and stay for one night in Camp Speicher and on the flight to FOB Danger in the morning. That night we slept in a container and I thank God so much for the favor. I couldn't thank him enough. I thank you father for showing me favor through these times, you have been so good to me, for I knew I may have messed up in my years of growing but God comes through when you least expect. I had to ask God was this my last favor? My heart answered with **NO** as long as you continue to praise me and lift me, honor me and spread my love the favors will continue. I felt a lift coming from me and feel asleep in the bosom of favor.

    Once again, I thought of home and what my then wife Darlene was actually doing, since our time zone was a day ahead of the normal time in the states. Due to the fact we had plans on our house to remodel the whole inside and out. I haven't had the chance to speak to her in three days during our convoy on the road, and I was sure she was worried about my travels.

In the morning we said our goodbyes to the rest of our people in our section, since we was not going to see them again for at least five months, and these were people we have grown accustomed while in Fort Dix. We arrived in FOB Danger early in the morning. Didn't know much of what was happening, because we were replacing the 1st ID, the Big Red One. This is a division in the military that is very well known throughout history. They have been in several wartime affairs, and we the 42nd ID were replacing them. We were to keep their standards and keep it going strong from where they left off at. Zechariah 3:7 (KJV) Thus saith the Lord of hosts; If thou wilt walk in my ways, and if thou wilt keep my charge, then thou shall also judge my house, and shalt also keep my courts, and I will give thee places to walk among these that stand by. Saying this since we were replacing 1st ID, we were allowed to do the same things they were doing, but we had to keep the same attitude they had and that is just what we did. We had to learn all those ways and certain things they did while on FOB Danger. Since my duty was refueling, my task was to service and keep the General's Aircraft refueled and prepped at all times. He had three aircrafts, and we were to keep them ready at all cost and under all conditions. My jobs also consisted of keeping track of all the fuel coming in and out of the area, and send them to my supervisor therefore; our numbers had to be correct. I took my mission and task pretty serious since I was dealing with fuel and aircrafts. I was doing my job there like I love the Lord, with all my might and soul. We were in a situation where we are the source of fuel for the aircrafts, you would think the enemy would try and get to the source of the aircrafts, which is fuel to fly. At which they tried you will hear about that later on. Living at the palace had its ups and downs, since we had to wait for the other unit to depart and go home so we can take over from where they left off at. Sleeping conditions were great we created our own room space there, the palace had marble every thing from steps to showers, circle staircases and high cathedral ceilings to stare at, handmade with very fine detail, perfect to the point. When I got to the palace I was certainly amazed at the building and art and then got interested in the history of this country and its ways. I wanted to learn more regarding Iraq and this war we was in. I went to sleep mostly every night thinking this is nice waking up in a palace, but it was not God's palace. This palace was done right thinking it was fine and it was, but not perfect. Little did I know it was an attraction and go getter for the insurgents, in other words a big target to take pot shots at with Mortars and RPG's which are rocket propelled guns.

After some of the safety briefings regarding the palace and its living situation and do's and don'ts. I began to wonder and pray more and more. At some point, I thought this maybe exciting since I love excitement and adventure. I was not going to let the stories of the palace get me stressed out and cannot perform the mission I was called to do there. Soon after that I began to fast and pray. Knowing that my favor was still fresh in the moment, my fasting will increase my faith in my work. I had fasted for five days since the first day of arriving and receiving the briefing. I knew what I had to fast for; safety, knowledge, respect of fellow soldiers, and guidance to my next level. In Matthew, Jesus speaks about fasting and what to fast for, just like Isaiah 58:4 (KJV) Behold, ye fast for strife and debate, and to smite with the fist of wickedness: ye shall not fast as ye do this day, to make your voice heard on high. He only fasted for strife and debate I was fasting for safety while in the presence of danger. These made me wonder why they called this FOB Danger does it have a history of dangerous acts and situations? I know

Camp Speicher has a history, Speicher was a Lt. in the navy who had flown over Iraq in the Desert Storm War and was shot down and never was found. Therefore, in honor of him they named a base after him. But FOB Danger is a bit different. Therefore, knowing this about Danger placed my faith on high. My heart became alert to my senses and they alerted everything else, reactions were on high, sense of smell was high, my eyes became adjusted to the dark so fast. Since it was dark, so dark you couldn't see anything. Therefore, getting to know the base was easy and kind of interesting for me. The aircrafts were always at the LZ, which is our landing zone. And we had to refuel them upon returning from a mission and prep them for the next. This was how the 1st ID soldiers informed us to do it. We became close to some of them and not so close to others. It seems like there are always something or someone who has the spirit of misleading people. We flew with the pilots on some missions, while General Taluto spoke to townships leaders and spokespersons, which was somewhat interesting to do. One time we flew up to Turkey which was north of Iraq and west of Iran, where they have the Kurdish people, wanting to be free of the Iraqi violence, they fed us this enormous feast, it was the strangest looking food I had ever seen and tasted, but they were the people of peace and love. We flew along the coast ridges and the mountains were beautiful reminded me of Mount Sinai, snow covered mountains that took the elevation high. These people lived in the hills of the Kurdish county and the elevation above sea level was so high it can make your nose bleed. All through the flying and the scenery it was a praying moment, thanking God for traveling mercy while flying amongst the sky, knowing we could easily get hit with a rocket, shot by the insurgents. God had his angels protecting us. Psalm 67:1 (KJV) God be merciful unto us, and bless us; and cause his face to shine upon us; Selah. I know He watches us. I felt the presence of God while flying, because I felt good and not afraid. I have often said and made promises to God during these times, like Lord get me through this and I will do anything you ask of me or Lord, I did this, thank you for that, and felt fine afterwards.

One day Joe my battle Buddy was missing his camera, and since it was him and I against the world there, what I mean is that we was there amongst the 1ˢᵗ ID (Infantry Division) guys. We were learning the ways, and hardly knew them and they did something quite foul to us. We had searched and searched all over for the camera and I finally told him, well choke it up as a lost and buy another one. Days went by and the camera popped up in the flight operations room. Joe came in saying he had found the camera. I said, "Good." Then we opened it to see if all the pictures were still on the camera, but lo and behold, there were other pictures on the camera, that was degrading for any human and disrespecting to us, and to top it off the faces were showing all involved. It was the guys from the other unit. Showing their genitals on the camera. Well, I got really upset, saying okay, "things are like this." I knew when you are praying for peace you actually do not get the peace you pray for, you get the piece of strength to sustain and keep you going, because you are about to get the opposite of the peace you prayed for. Psalm 71:15-17 (KJV) My mouth shall shew forth thy righteousness and thy salvation all the day; for I know not the numbers thereof. I didn't know how many people I was up against in this situation Verse 16, I will go in the strength of the Lord God: I will make mention of thy righteousness, even of thine only. I went to them with God on my side using strength in my mind. Verse 17, O God, thou hast taught me from my youth: and hitherto have I declared thy wondrous works. God has really taught me when I was younger how to be tough and handle hard situations and approach them with unknowing strength. I went in and asked the guys in the flight operations room. Who did this? Because leave it up to Joe a fight was breaking out, and we didn't need that. So, me being his NCO and we being from the same company, I decided to step up and speak to the other soldiers who had done this damage. I was calm and insisted to know who had done what, because if they did not tell; I was taking it to their supervisor or higher. I was so angry with those guys and here we are in another country with this nonsense going on. They claimed it was a joke but to me that was not a joke, and I got to the bottom of the joke quick, since I was a sergeant and the person who did the joke was a lower rank then me. I used the pen, which was mightier than me hitting him. God had showed me direction through the whole time on how to handle those guys. From then on I knew this wasn't going to be a picnic in the palace. Here I was thinking **"YEAH"** the palace we got it made, but it is the people that make the environment we live in. Wherever you go something's may be array and out of place, but it is the people that make it. God had blessed us with endurance and sacrifice to make the right decisions under certain circumstances that is never out of control.

After we got settled in the palace and begin to know FOB Danger and its whereabouts and happenings. I found out the church was active and joined quickly and became active in the church choir and all. Then, I actually really knew this was it. Knowing God in all countries, we had bible studies, choir rehearsals and doing everything like back home. Church made people feel like they were being part of something for God. I loved the choir; it consisted of people from all over the country and United States. We were from all the states and just think we were singing for the Lord. We became the 42nd ID Church Choir, complete with a band and all. Now let me explain, we did not know each other at all therefore, once again the attitudes flared at each other, but we knew what that was amongst us. We did songs that reminded all of us of something at home. God's emotions would come through and the spirit of the Lord would rise to the occasion at any given time. We did not have to worry about a place to have service; since we were replacing another service we just fitted right in. The place we had was a giant palace which had this huge auditorium and we never found out who the palace belonged to. The palace could have been Saddam's son's house, but this palace had everything a gym, spiral staircases and all. We just happen to have a young Pastor (from Missouri) who was an awesome blessed man of God. He would touch subjects like the pastors back home; we were all teachers among teachers. The pastor that was elected was also an officer of the military (Captain Frelick) awesome brother in the word. It was like God had placed him here for the purpose of teaching soldiers how to deal with the feeling of being away from home, how to cope with God and that is what we did. He had Bible studies, choir rehearsals, everything like we did back home. This Brother brought us to another level in the Word, when everyone was feeling down, this brother was there to uplift your spirits and keep you up. Colossians 1 verse 28 reads, Whom we preach warning every man, and teaching every man in all wisdom; that we may present every man perfect in Christ Jesus. Therefore, we became the teachers of the teacher. We had gatherings amongst people, studies, and prayer nights, which lasted for hours. This was where I became so avid in the word I got involved in almost everything going on around the FOB. Our services were bringing people from other FOB's to see our choir sing, we wasn't the best but we put our hearts in it.

We knew the Devil was up to tactics when one day we were having a blessed service and the lights went out completely. That did not stop brother Frelick, he kept preaching in the pitched dark as long as people heard his voice they was fine. The lights stayed out for at least 30 to 40 minutes. I'm sure every soldier reading this book who was over there at this time remembers the lights going out. God was in the place ministering to us as well. Psalm 46 verses 1 and 2 states, God is our refuge and strength, a very present help in trouble. Therefore we will not fear, though the earth be removed, and through the mountains be carried into the midst of the sea. All I was thinking was is everyone thinking the way I am. That was being in a calm state of mind, and everyone was calm, shucks! If we were back home and the lights went out it would have been mayhem and bedlam in other words, bonkers! The peace was within each of us there even the congregation; the people did not panic at all. When the lights came back on Lord, we rejoiced like no other but even louder. It seemed like fun, we defeated an obstacle point blank. This was all God doing His best, because there wasn't any shortage or anything they just came on, no one had to flip a switch, they just came on. This is what I am talking about being in the mist of God. Psalm 48:14 (KJV) For this God is our God, for ever and ever: He will be our guide unto death. As the service continued, we enjoyed the lights being out.

I would tell you now, we comforted each other through some times of despair we did not have to know each other but we found each others hearts. Some soldiers on the choir were sad, some were mad and the women would be up tight. Some of the men were consoling the women through their troubles, but this is actually when God shows up. Jesus speaks about friends in John 15:13 (NKJV) Greater love has no one than this, than to lay down one's life for his friends. Now let me explain, we are in war time situation laying down my life for this person was already at stake. Now I am saving someone in all conditions, actually speaking to someone in a time of trouble. That was one circumstance and then war was another. So, now place them together and you get an array of problems, and since they are your friend and fellow soldier and then worships God with you; you tend to care with the love of God. The sad feelings drift in you, you tend to feel the person completely, and then you feel it lift out. One soldier I became close to, whose wife lost their first child and he could not go home nor could he call. We sat and prayed because he felt like doing things to people that was crazy and could get into trouble for. Therefore, I prayed Psalm 17 verse 1, Hear the right, O Lord, attend to my cry, give ear unto my prayer, that goeth not out of feigned lips. This was my Psalms to reach for this soldier, and I felt his pain. It was the pain of joy, people don't understand you have a joyful pain, which can hurt but you feel good and blessed, when you reach out and minister to someone. Therefore, I felt his pain and felt good about it. I knew the brother was in a crisis and needed assistance spiritually and I was there. I read in the bible Nahum 1 verse 7, The Lord is good, a stronghold in the day of trouble; and He knowth them who trust in Him. I asked the young soldier if he had trusted in the Lord, his reply was "he can" if you can you will. Because once you can do something, you are showing your will to create a positive atmosphere with God in it. I created another Psalms in someone else through my love for his situation.

(Blackhawk's Flying Over Land)
EXPLORING THE LANDS BEFORE ENTERING TERRITORY!

CHAPTER 5

FRESH FIRE

Knowing the connection from home was in my spirit, I was feeling renewed. Psalm 40:3 (NKJV) He has put a new song in my mouth-Praise to our God; many will see it and fear, and will trust the Lord. Matthew 26:28 (KJV) For this my blood of the new testament, which is shed for many for the remission of sins. Colossians 3:10 (KJV) And have put on the new man, which is renewed in knowledge after the image of him that created him. Feeling like new flame, like at my home church "THE CATHEDRAL OF FRESH FIRE". God was always present there and you do not always feel it you see it. My spark of flame was lit in Iraq, everyone started to get involved in bible studies, Rehearsals, gathering and so forth. 2 Corinthians 5:17 (KJV) Therefore if man be in Christ, he is a new creature: old things are passed away; behold, all things are become new. Nevertheless, for me the Fresh Fire (new) attitude was regaining strength amongst the congregation and choir. The knowledge I was gaining was helping me get through most of my trials and circumstances. Fresh is new and Iraq was new to many of us. We actually was walking on biblical grounds, realizing this history produced a new kind of spirit in me. I was elated by the new spirit in me.

- Eden was in Iraq – Genesis 2:10-14
- Adam & Eve were created in Iraq – Genesis 2:7-8
- Satan First recorded appearance IN Iraq – Genesis 3:1-6
- Abraham came from a city in Iraq – Genesis 11:31 and Acts 7:2-4
- The events of the book of Esther took place in Iraq – Esther

In addition, these are just a few; the name Iraq means country with deep roots. Indeed Iraq is a country with deep roots and is a very significant county in the bible. The word Mesopotamia means between the two rivers, the Tigris and the Euphrates Rivers. Where I was tasked out with the 42nd division, was right on the banks of the Tigris River. Many think Iraq was an Oil rich nation with an evil dictator for thirty some odd years. However, the country is rich in history; Mesopotamia, which is now called Iraq, was the cradle of civilization. Finding out this history blessed my heart therefore I can bless others. Moreover, that was just a small hint of Iraqi history. YOU SEE! I felt fresh like the first time the Holy Spirit touched me. Pastor Creamer told me this would happen. I cried uncontrollably and ran around the church, thanking God for blessing me, allowing me to feel his presence live all day everyday and thanking him for touching me. That was FRESH FIRE. The longer the days seemed to me the more active I got in doing sessions of the Purpose Driven Life by Rick Warren that went on for two to three months holding classes and watching tapes of Purpose Driven Life. That was very exciting to most of us. One of the most exciting things that happened to me was when I finally had leave time, meaning it was time to relax from this situation. I arranged for me and my then wife to travel to Germany and see the sites; I had two weeks of leave awarded to me. I had gone for a day or so and then picked her up and we flew to Germany. This was a military resort for soldiers on leave called the EDELWEISS. We went to Bavaria seen the castles and all. Nevertheless, God speaks to you wherever you are at.

Sometimes you have to know when God is speaking to you, whether it is coming from someone else or something, Gods speaks! It can be soft or loud, as long as it is heard; I was being spoken to and was reacting to it somewhat funny, because it was not known to me. In other words, I am saying I was being told something and was not paying any attention. We had several incidents occurring right before my eyes. My battle Buddy Joe Jennings, he came to the palace with me and was assigned on the task, well he kept badgering me about going to the PX (store) to pick up a few items, mind you, we had to walk seven miles, I was tired that day and it was 130 degrees with the weather. I did not want to go anywhere, I just wanted to relax on my bed and read or play a game, you know just take it easy for that day. However, he kept bothering me about going, repeatedly, until I just said, "Okay, come on". Therefore, I had to gather my things (helmet, weapon, Kevlar vest which weigh about 15 pounds) and dealt with the heat, walking the 7 miles, laughing and joking. There and back took several hours, but when we returned the road to our palace was blocked off and the activity level was High, MP (Military Police) swarming all over the place. We had asked what happened, WE HAVE BEEN HIT BY A MORTAR ROCKET. Joe and I just looked at each other with this look of anger and surprised mixed. The rocket had sharply entered the building and out the other side. I just backed up from the crowd walked away with my eyes slowly tearing to myself, praising God and all His Glory. However, another thought crossed my mind, that we actually got hit, that is really close to home for me. Psalm 39:1 (KJV) I said, I will take heed to my ways that I sin not with my tongue: I will keep my mouth bridle, while the wicked is before me. I walked away thanking God for my safety and will continue to lift him up. I found an area to be alone and let God minister to me like no other. I thought about my fellow soldiers in Kirkuk, just north of where I was. Were they going through the same thing? Psalm 25:21 (KJV) Let integrity and uprightness preserve me; for I wait on thee. We needed protection spiritually and if they were not praying, I am praying for them. I had placed myself in the position of Jabez when he prayed, "bless me Lord only my friends and me." Every time I left the building, I would see the damage done. Shucks! I slept on the second floor of that building and it went and exited out the other side. Scary stuff. I prayed so much at night, due to the fact rockets could come and hit as we slept.

Sometimes I did not even care; I was protected by my faith in God. There were times I would sit outside my deck room and make room amongst the stars at night, place myself high and ask God to change my ways and to help me be a better person in all my ways, I wanted to be a better husband, father, friend, and child of God. I knew I have not always been saved; my forgiving stage goes back some twenty odd years. As I lay my head at night another rocket can easily hit us. Being on my knees every night became normal for me. I wanted to do so while I was there, and do it the right way. Psalm 40:11 (KJV) Withhold not thou thy tender mercies from me, O Lord: Let thy loving kindness and thy truth continually preserve me. Therefore when it was time to return home; that look of a new man would show upon me. It seems the more I thought about the new Ken the more incidents occur right before, like saying "Like what I can do?" I started to realize this was real.

During our game one-night explosions just happening just 500 feet from the courts, the people started scattering all over running around, it was pandemonium out there. I was acting as if I was superman or something, standing there in the mist of trouble. I knew I looked somewhat weird, but I was praying. I did the casual thing, kept walking, and kept my eyes open, I did not want to knock anybody down, but it got pretty nuts out there. It got to the point where if we heard an explosion we were used to it (even during basketball.)

I am serious, God is amazing and does things right even if it's scolding you Psalm 5:10 (KJV) Destroy thou them O God; let them fall by their own counsels; cast them out in the multitude of their transgressions; for they have rebelled against thee. I was feeling like God was scolding me sometimes, if I was doing or saying the wrong things. I know I came short of the glory getting upset and angry, feeling like hurting people, I ask myself why I am feeling this way. Maybe it was time to go home! I started working out and hitting the gym to relieve me of the feeling of pain. Then, the gym became a place of refuge for me also. I began to feel some sort of way about home and what was going on, because I was overseas and did not know the aspects of the home life with my then wife. All I knew I needed to be home because attitudes were flying high with us. We were bickering on the phone and that rather disturbed me while over there. My sense of being a husband was lost then, my wife was asking me for a divorce on the phone and I was thousands of miles away…why? Then, I wondered God will direct this whole thing because I couldn't figure it out. Proverb 3:5-6 (KJV) Trust in the Lord with all thine heart; and lean not unto thine own understanding. In all thy ways acknowledge him, and he shall direct thy paths. The funds were alright and the bills were getting paid. My house was getting remodeled and I am sure she was happy. I was getting worried and frustrated and seeing the explosions outside my window was not helping at all. Casting my cares on God became somewhat hard to do! I wanted to spend the night in the church there. In addition, lay right on the floor until service started. Romans 8:28 (KJV) And we know that all things work together for good to them that love God, to them who are called according to his purpose. It would have been worth it. Our tournament was ending and there was a winner out of all this. Nevertheless, we were all conquerors placed under this country, whether we were there to work or play a sport we were conquerors in our own way. We gave out the trophies that we received from the states and everyone was happy. We scheduled to fit the commanding General in the plan to say a few words of encouragement to the soldiers. It was a blessed night for everyone; we had music, food and the love of God in the atmosphere. I knew we had completed a great task for the morale of the soldiers.

Soon the news was around we were being sent home, some were sad and some were glad and overjoyed with the fact of going home. As the word had spread around the FOB that we were due to go home, it seemed like time had actually slowed down, and we were catching up. I started to try to reminisce on home. Thinking about smalls things that may not seem anything to anybody else for instance, I haven't seen birds fly in a flock or group in so long, I was beginning to think if they still flew together, the water in the lake was always so dark green. I would probably bug out if I saw a clear pond or blue water. These were just a small amount of things to think about. Like taking baths, we were taking showers for 18 months, I need to sit and soak my body for at least two hours. Taking showers was a crazy thing, the water was very unpredictable. First you get the wave of hot water and all of a sudden it is cool as December and sometimes green. Nevertheless, the thought of going home was in my spirit and dwelling in the air.

All I knew now is that God had supplied my needs and had given me the strength to get through hills of tribulation I faced while in Iraq. I kept thanking the Lord saying, I was able to get through anything. Read the book of 2 Corinthians. As long as I had the Lords word embedded in my soul. Therefore, at one point I was feeling somewhat good in this thing called spiritual empowerment of one's self. Maybe we all thought getting here was going to be hard to do and stay for the duration of time allowed. Then the reality of going home kicked in and we had to prepare for that as well. Being supplied with a new kind of strength Philippians 4:19 (KJV) But my God shall supply all your need according to his riches in glory by Christ Jesus. That can never be forsaken or forgotten. So now, our date was set in stone, we were returning home on November 25, 2005, but shucks! That was still a few months away. Moreover, work still had to be completed and tasks had to be done, reports and mortars still had to be seen, explosions still had to be heard, and dealing with knuckleheaded people was still on my list. I had received a new soldier to finish out the rest of our tour; because my battle buddy Joe Jennings went home and did not come back. I wonder if the rest of our section heard the news, I was sure they did, SFC Shortlidge was excellent in putting out news, and he had SGT. Malone, SGT. Hamilton, SGT. Jones, SGT. Milner, SSGT. Miller, SGT. Allen, SPC. Reno Reali, and the rest of the POL crew. If they did hear the news that everybody was going home, we would all be together again. Even SPC.Woods who would read all the scary vampires books around and scares himself to sleep. However, until then we still had duties to do, I still had to report to SFC. Hicks for all the fuel we were receiving and giving out.

KEEPING TIME TO MYSELF

CHAPTER 6

COMPLETING THE END

Our mission was never undone and so was my faith in God. As long as we continued to move forward as the completion was nearing the faith was cheerful. 2 Timothy 1:7 (KJV) For God hath not given us the spirit of fear; but power, and of love, and of a sound mind. We were no longer afraid to do our tasks and yes, it was getting close, we were packing two months out and praying for it to come sooner. Things were still arising around us as if the Iraqis knew it was time for us soldiers to leave because explosions began everywhere, some were close and some were far. We had a Mortar round fly right over our heads and skip the propeller of the aircraft we operated, and hit a tree. It was nuts that day. The General was about to go out on his daily mission, I had just refueled his aircraft and was waiting for him to arrive so that I can leave. It was a nice clear afternoon day, temperature was 130 degrees and I was used to this now. We had a lot of activity around the LZ (Land Zone) that day. I was in charge of two fuels trucks and those mortars hit in the general area. In addition, it came just as the CG (Commanding General) was arriving to get on the aircraft, like if they knew something about him arriving. However, when the rocket hit; the General and his staff seen it and ran behind the fuel truck, I said, "NO, not here;" "You have to move from here." The commotion level was somewhat high; they were supposed to hide in the bunkers where it was safe. Not behind a fuel truck, I'll tell you, that day was crazy, MP's came over, investigators was all over the place. That tree burned for a few hours, but that was a real narrow escape for all of us. Tension was high that day. The General took the rest of the day off.

This also would give me a chance to catch up on reading or just relaxing thinking about going home. I wanted to be a different person when I returned home. As time went by, I knew that it did not depend on me, it depended on God and what was the situation like upon returning. I want to be one way and I am another way towards my family, which was kind of shaky for me. I did not know if the wife would like my attitude towards things. All I can do is pray for guidance, "Lord provide me the right words and the right attitude," because I was reentering back into the world from which I derived from and it may not be the same. Being away from home placed my heart in God's hands; due to all the situations I surpassed, I had only God to thank for the overcoming. When I felt I could not go on something had pushed me to go on. 2 Corinthians 12:9 (KJV) And he said unto me, My grace is sufficient for thee: for my strength is made perfect in weakness. Most gladly therefore will I rather glory in my infirmities, that the power of Christ may rest upon me. I was moving on without knowing it and making progress at it to. When I would feel like "this is crazy and I cannot make it here in the desert living amongst the bombs and explosions and attitudes from other people." Psalm 91:15 (KJV) He shall call upon me, and I will answer him: I will be with him in trouble; I will deliver him, and honor him. God made it possible for me to walk in the way of the righteous and be safe with all eyes open. Our time was nearing to exit this country with grace, but to exit with grace we had to somewhat do a back step and follow the way we came in. In other words, we were all tasked out to different FOB's from the Speicher Base Camp. Therefore, we had to return to Speicher and that is when the reunion began.

Basically, we were setting up to go home and I was actually thinking did I change in any aspect, a person does not know if he has changed unless he has been put in the same situation that made him change, change comes by action and realizing the walk you want to take. In addition, me being away I was really being put aside for God to work on but under certain channels (the war). I knew I was being worked on while in Iraq. God worked on Moses in Exodus 3 taking everything away from him and bring him to the mountain to actually speak to him and give him the way. Moses had everything in Egypt, he was next in line for Pharaoh, but God had other plans. God casted him out of Egypt not Pharaoh, he had nothing to do with Moses getting out. It was the alone time Moses was getting from God to make a change in his life. He was in the mountains for forty years all alone with God. Don't you think that would change anybody? Even if they were in prison for forty years, a change has to occur. Jesus had alone time with God in the mountains as well, fasting and praying while all the time being tempted by the devil. Read Matthew 4 verses 1 through 25. He spent forty days in the wilderness wrestling with temptation and conquered it. I spent 180 days in changing me and God working through me, I figured like this 4 goes into 180 days 45 times, which actually brings me close to the 40 days of seclusion with God. Forty-five days is what I come up with. Moreover, my change has come within me, and my walk with God shows to others and is felt in my own heart. Therefore, my alone time with God in Iraq and all I have experienced was presenting itself out. But only shown to those who experienced the same things I have, not seen to those before I changed. I said to myself, "Everyone would go home a new person, and who is going to see this change?" Our time was winding down to a few months but work had to be done to go home. The packing was crazy for us; even though we were leaving most of our equipment there for the other units to use. I could not wait to see our fellow soldiers that were in Kirkuk, it was a glorious reunion for us. We all met back in Tent City; Tent City is where they placed all the tents for the troops to sleep in. My section the (POL) had our own tent. We were so happy to be back in; because Speicher, is where everyone else was and knowing the fact we were on our way back home.

Was this over? I guess so, because when we hit Speicher which is our base camp, there was no more bombing going on or Mortars coming our way. Therefore, I was thinking, was this over for us? God has kept me through it all and I was grateful, so grateful. The thing with Speicher is that that camp was so dark, I mean so dark, you could not see your hand before you. In addition, the thought of a person walking up on you can actually hurt somebody. Nevertheless, we stayed there for a few weeks still preparing to leave. My prayers kept me strong talking to God every night was an amazing thing to experience, and getting a response back was even more mind blowing to me. Therefore, everything worked itself out for me. If anyone knew angels I found them in me, watching me and keeping me well. I did not need an ordinary love because an ordinary love just wouldn't do. I received the love of God in my heart to its extent and that was special to me. I was longing to be in His presence and place to comfort me while on my trip home. I did not figure out if anyone else was feeling the same way I was. I guess I was doing my own thing with God, that is when I found a definite friend in my God, a friend I could carry with me, speak with me, and honor with me. Jesus knows all my struggles everyone of them even while I was on duty and with God on my side, I was strong enough to face my foes. The angels were watching me keeping me from harm, danger and hurt. In addition, this is an angel I had to strive to know and I had all the time in my life. This actually took me back when I was like seven years old, I remember my grandmother telling my mother, "He is going to be something someday" I actually heard this from her own mouth. Nevertheless, being young I did not know I was going to end up in Iraq thirty-nine years later. Going home really made me think back over my life, and I saw all the things God done for me. I had been through danger, heartaches and troubles. I thank the Lord, He rescued me. I could have been dead and gone, but the Lord spared my life. Now, I can say that I am still here and it's by the grace of God. I was pouring my love out right there in the mist of the people around me. The Lord had brought me through sickness, sadness and suffering, I thank the Lord, He blessed me. I could have lost the faith and I could have fallen from His grace. Now, I can say that I am still here and it is by the grace of God. I never would have made it this far without the guidance of God. I can say He brought me all the way, through by His grace I am saved. Attitudes were different from most of the people I have not seen in months. The experience is great and astonishing, but nothing was more experiencing than experiencing the love of my God. There is no greater love, than the love God had for us. The soldiers were singing and partying through the night, they were giving praise in their own way. Psalm 100:1 (KJV) Make a joyful noise unto the Lord, all ye lands. Rejoicing was mandatory for everyone there. Still our missions were going on, but by that time the new units were coming in to relieve us but to see our relief was happy, because we had to show them the ropes and provide them with the equipment we were using and show them the do's and don'ts of the base camp. It was time to go home, after spending several more weeks in Speicher we knew it was almost time to head to Kuwait then the states. GOD HAS BEEN GOOD TO US…and I was so grateful and full of joy knowing this was not really over because I still had time to do in the military, but this was just a little way of making things happen in the way God wanted it. Which was to return us home without any injuries? The only injury I had been making it home and things was not the same. I complete this scribe in the way God had me to complete this. I cannot say the prayer is the same from the beginning, because it is stronger than before. The intensity is not the same, I have become more sensible, more loving towards things I do not have, more caring in the eyes of God, more giving to people, but do people see my love toward caring , do people see my care for God, do people see my caring. NO, but as long as the Lord, my God is watching over me with a watchful eye, I will forever be in His presence. No matter where I am at in Iraq, or in the United States of America, God is forever seeing the being within me. Being that our time was actually shorter than I expected it to be, heading home was a mandatory aspect in my life at the time. The roll downhill was happening to me and everyone around me. I knew I had not completely lived my Psalms in my life, because I still had to return home. No one can completely live out his or her Psalms because there is always another day coming in that person's life. God has a way of blessing people through the Psalms of their lives. Every day is a trial lived out through a Psalms. Mine happened to be lived out in Iraq for that period. Was my mission done? I asked myself, because we were returning home. I would not ever know, because everyday was completed with something to ponder on. An individuals Psalm can go on for an extended amount of time of their life, even when they have past on; because someone will remember them and maybe write about it. I just happen to write about my trials therefore everyone will understand the Psalms of their lives. My thoughts created a sensor that connected with God to create the Psalms.

Going home opened a window for another Psalms in my life which I have dealt with in Iraq. Saying that since I knew I was heading home I didn't know what was coming to me. Therefore, I had to pray for everything to be peaceful and praying for it to be the same. We all knew and understood it would not be the same. I cannot say I was feeling like David when he wrote Psalms and some chapters. I say my sorrows and happiness brought them out in the open. It brought out my Psalms of sorrows and my Psalms of happiness, which created a spirit in me to deal with the attitudes forthcoming at home. I was open and very sensitive to everyone upon returning home. I thought maybe no one would understand me and things would not be the same. I had time to think and pray on a constant basis while over there, I placed myself in God's hands every night and I thought I may not be able do the same when I get home. But then another realization kicked in, if not, I will have another Psalms to continue on. One more which was wide, meaning wide enough to receive all God's blessings. My Psalms is meant for everyone to see they have Psalms as well. They are supposed to be praised by God as long as it is from God. You have to be very thankful to pray to a wonderful God, then your Psalms will be lifted for Gods blessings. I thank God for blessing me with Psalms that will bless someone else. I thank God for the trials and tribulations to create a Psalms within me. To me Psalms means continuous blessings, meaning you will be blessed as long as you strengthen yourself with God's word. His word will dwell within and you can create a Psalms that comes from within. I do not know how to end this book, because so much has been created in me to present Psalms. Psalm 89:34 (KJV) My covenant will I not break, nor alter the thing that is gone out of my lips. I had a covenant to keep with God and that was my Psalms. That is how it is going to be continuous by keeping a covenant with God. God honors covenants; God honors prayers that extends pass Psalms. I am asking those who read this Psalms bless yourself with your very own Psalms and live an honorable life seen by God. Your Psalms are blessed by God and seen through the eyes of others, on how your life has surpassed the hard and rough times through Psalms. Your Psalms is your life, my Psalms is my life.

42ID CHURCH CHOIR

IN FRONT OF THE PALACE

AT THE LANDING ZONE

PREPARING FOR A MISSION WITH GOD BY MY SIDE

MEDIATING TO THE FATHER

GOD'S VIEW OF FOREIGN BLESSINGS AND INSIGHT

THE DESERT OF IRAQ

DAWN APPROACHING, WE ARE RESTING AND PRAYING

GLORY FROM GOD SHINES FROM ABOVE

www.ingramcontent.com/pod-product-compliance
Lightning Source LLC
Chambersburg PA
CBHW032017290426
44109CB00013B/692